The Storm Of Becoming

A journey through the chaos of Youth

Saumitra Srivastava

BookLeaf Publishing
India | USA | UK

Made with ❤ on the BookLeaf Publishing Platform
www.bookleafpub.in
www.bookleafpub.com

Dedication

To the wandering hearts,
the dreamers with tired eyes,
the souls caught between becoming and belonging—
This is for you.
For every tear you never showed,
for every hope you still hold.

Preface

This book is a storm.
A storm of questions, dreams, heartbreaks,
and awakenings.
Each poem in these pages was written during
moments of quiet chaos—when youth felt too
heavy, and the world moved too fast.
They are not just words.
They are fragments of my becoming.
In the blur of responsibilities, expectations,
and silent wars with self, I wrote to breathe.
I wrote to remember.
And now, I write to share.
If you've ever felt lost, uncertain, too much or
not enough—
May these poems remind you: you're not
alone in the storm.

Acknowledgements

To the ones who saw light in my darkness,
and silence in my noise—thank you.
To my family, who stood quietly behind me,
even when I couldn't explain the whirlwind
inside—your love was my anchor.
To the friends who listened, laughed, stayed,
and held space for my words—this book
carries your warmth.
To every unspoken goodbye, unfinished
chapter, and unhealed scar—thank you for
becoming poetry.
And to you, dear reader—thank you for
holding my storm with your hands.
You make the chaos worth writing.

1. The Youth I Never Knew

A lifetime, they say - a fleeting spark,
Youth so bright, yet cold and dark.
Dreams like embers, fade away,
No one told me, nights feel this way.

Even in laughter, echoes remain,
Heavy hearts walk through rain.
Lost in the noise, yet all alone,
Chasing faces I've never known.

Four walls listen to the words I hide,
Talking to mirrors, searching inside.
And if this is life, then I've learned to see,
A smile is better than words can be.

No bandage now, I heal with time,
Turning my scars into painted lines.
I fall, I break, but I don't stay,
This fire inside will light my way.

Through silent wars, I stand tall,
No one to catch me, when I fall.
Lessons carved in every scar,
They shape me who I truly are.

Fighting shadows, burning bright,
Carrying stars into the night.
A restless torch, a fearless flame,
I rise again, I call my name.

This age has taught me, war never ends,
Battle after battle, then rise again.
Take today or let it go,
The war of life is all I know.

2. Don't Blame, Just Believe

It's easy to blame fate,
Your parents, your past, or a twist of state.
But ask yourself—deep inside,
Are you stuck in a lie you tried to hide?

Dreams don't grow from greed or ease,
They need faith and endless belief.
Just imagining won't make them real,
Hard work is what makes them sealed.

So, hold on, don't give in,
Your dreams will come, just stay within.
They never leave, they never die,
Have patience—one day, you'll fly.

3. I Hope This Email Finds You Well

Another dawn, the screen aglow,
A flood of emails starts to flow.
Unread lines in endless streams,
Tasks and meetings, deadlines, dreams.

Click, refresh, the same old phrase,
A robotic wish in digital haze.
But pause—what if it's true today?
What if this hope lights up your way?

Each message sent, a story spun,
A task assigned, a job well done.
A silent nod, a bridge of trust,
A sign your work is worth so much.

So, take a breath, sit up tall,
You matter here, you do it all.
If no one's said it, hear it now—
You're doing great, take a bow.

Now go, reply, press send with grace,
And conquer your inbox, your rightful place.

4. Are You Alive… or Just Breathing?

Everyone says,
"If you're breathing, you're alive."
But have you ever felt that breath?
Moving through your veins like a quiet river,
And smiled… just because you're still here?

The light in your eyes may fade with time,
Maybe in a few short years.
But the dreams behind those eyes?
They'll only live…If you keep moving.
Because this path,
This deep ocean you're swimming in,
It's yours. Only yours.

Has your breath ever hit you like a storm?
Shaken your soul, And whispered…
Wake up… you're still alive.

When you're running fast through life,

And one day, you stop... too tired to move,
Listen,
Listen to your breath.
Each gasp, each sound, each rhythm,
Will cry out loud,
To the world,
To you:
You still want to live.
Maybe that's why...You are still alive.

You close your eyes and fall asleep,
But you wake up again, alive.
Have you ever asked yourself—
What keeps you going?

Is it the memories of yesterday?
Or the hopes for tomorrow?
Is it the fire of a dream you haven't dared to chase?

Because without dreams,
Without something to believe in,
To fight for,
To wake up for—
Are you really alive...
Or just breathing?

5. Dazed. Dreaming. Determined.

Some walk-through youth, with a dazed kind of gaze,
Lost in the noise, just drifting through days.
They scroll, they sigh, they follow the crowd,
Their inner voice? Not too loud.
They live, but not quite feel alive,
Surviving, not seeking ways to thrive.
Questions echo, but answers hide,
And they don't know what burns inside.

Some dream, and oh—they dream so wide,
Castles in clouds, hearts full of pride.
They see the stars, they feel the fire,
But stop just short of climbing higher.
They talk of change, of paths untread,
But leave those words unsaid in bed.
They're not lazy, just lost in thought,
Fighting battles they never fought.

And then—there are the few who burn,

Who fail, then fall, but rise and learn.
They dream too, but while they walk,
They build their world, not just talk.
They wake before the world begins,
They chase their loss, they earn their wins.
Eyes clear, with no time to waste,
Fueled by fire, moved by taste.

Dazed... and time will slip away,
Dreaming... and you might just stay.
But determined...
You'll carve your way.
Through storm and stone—you *won't* delay.

So, ask yourself in this fleeting phase,
Are you lost, just staring into space?
Are you dreaming with no end in sight?
Or are you *rising*, ready to fight?

6. A War Within

In the depths of my quiet mind,
A war begins of a different kind.
Between the mind of my thoughts and soul,
A silent battle, taking its toll.

There's a noise I feel but cannot say,
Only my tired eyes give it away.
And a thought that lingers deep inside,
Keeps clashing with the peace I hide.

I'm at odds with what I used to choose,
Now in my heart, there's quiet bruise.
The night slips by with eyes still wide,
And sleep, it's nowhere left to hide.

Don't know why rest no longer stays,
Why silence speaks in sleepless ways.
And yet again, with morning's light,
I fake a smile, I wear it right.

There's fear that rests beneath my skin,
Because dreams now wait for work to begin.
And the child who once dreamt without a care,
Now learns that **life is rarely fair.**

7. My Voice Must Rise Again

Every moment, my heart pounds,
Echoing the weight of troubles around.

Every moment, my eyes flickers,
Clouded by the fear of what lingers.

Every moment, my breath turns heavy,
Crushed beneath the burden of worry.

Every moment, my ears retreat,
Dreading the echoes of defeat.

Every moment, my lips seal tight,
Choked by the silence of fright.

Every moment, my feet recoil,
Hoping to escape the storm's turmoil.

Every moment, my hands withdraw,

Shying away from chances I saw.

But how long?
How long will my heart beat—without joy?
How long will my eyes blink—without dreams?
How long will my breath race—without chasing victories?
How long will my ears shut—without hearing cheers?
How long will my lips close—without speaking truth?
How long will my feet tremble—without scaling walls of success?
How long will my hands hesitate—without lifting the fallen?

How long will I ignore?
How long will I hide?
How long will my voice remain unheard?

Until I change, the world remains the same.
Until I rise, no storm will carry my name.

To make, to create, to change.
To help, to feel, to express.
My voice must break the chains,
My voice must rise again!

8. Yet He Kept Walking

He stared at life's sharp-edged track,
But never once did he look back.
With a fading smile, he played the game,
Through joy or pain, he stayed the same.

He bore the silence, loud and raw,
Yet moved ahead without a flaw.
At every turn, new foes would rise,
But he moved on, with steady eyes.

He had a hope to live life bright,
To chase the smiles in others' light.
At every pause, new paths would show,
With storms besides, he'd choose to go.
The road was rough, the climb was steep,
But still, he walked, with dreams to keep.

There was a high in every dream,
Each golden ray a glowing beam.
Each moment tied a thread so new,

Each step a vision to pursue.
The journey tough, the will was true,
But still he walked, as dreamers do.

On thorny roads, his feet were bare,
Temptations whispered false affair.
The ladder cracked beneath his feet,
Yet he stood up, refused defeat.
The world was hard, the climb unfair,
But he kept moving, unaware.

Yes, he walked and walked again,
Through darkest nights, through deepest pain.
The world may change, the light may dim,
But he kept walking, and, **That was him.**

9. Dreams with Open Eyes

I fear the night, not for its shade,
But for the dreams that start to fade.
They bloom in dark, they break at dawn,
And by the morning—they're all gone.

They say if dawn dreams come alive,
Then I just pray—I'll survive to strive.
So every morning, I make one plea:
"Let there be one more dawn for me."

The dreams I lose, I chase awake,
'Cause open-eye dreams are hard to take.
They burn, they bite, they leave a mark,
They haunt you more than dreams in dark.

With closed eyes, I find some peace,
But open them, and the wars don't cease.
With shut eyes, I'm Arjun—strong and brave,
Open them—I'm Abhimanyu in a cave.

I fall, I rise, I fight, I bend,
I push, I bleed, I break, I mend.
I reach so close, then lose it all,
I climb so high—just to fall.

But open eyes show truth, not lies,
No painted wings, no pretty skies.
They show the scars, the fight, the flame,
Dreams with open eyes—they call your name.

They show the war, they never yield—
They make you stand on your own battlefield.

10. Sheltered Too Long

I have just one complaint, dear Mom and Dad,
For everything else, I'm truly glad.
You gave me love, a roof, a dream—
The safest world I'd ever seen.

But maybe, once, just once, you should've let me fall,
Let me scrape my knees, let me crawl.
Had you stepped back while I tried to rise,
I might've seen life through my own eyes.

Beneath your care, I stayed in shade,
Never learned how sunlight's made.
And now the world burns with its heat,
While I stumble, barefoot, on life's street.

The journey hurts, the nights are long,
The road feels rough, though I act strong.
But see, I'm walking, not with ease,
Yet slowly learning how to breathe.

I know you did it all with love,
A shield around me, hand in glove.
But strength, you see, grows best in pain,
And sunshine comes with its fair share of rain.

So, thank you, truly, for all you gave,
For every time you came to save.
But next time, let me lose the fight,
So I may learn to find my light.

11. Worshipped, Yet Unknown

They worshipped you in sculpted stone,
But your true soul remained unknown.
They praised your grace, adorned your name,
Yet never looked beyond the frame.

Your feet they touched with deep respect,
But your real worth they still neglect.
The truth you hold, the strength you show,
A silent storm they'll never know.

You wear so many forms with grace,
Kali's fire, Durga's face.
Yet still the world just looks away,
Afraid of all you have to say.

Let them hear, let them see,
You are the storm, the flame, the sea.
Not just a name in whispered prayer,
But strength and power, beyond compare.

12. Breaking Free

They say, "You're a pretty bird, so mild,
Stay in the cage, be soft, be styled."

But tell them loud: I'm born to soar,
A fierce eagle, I'm so much more.
No bars, no bounds, no lines for me,
I'm meant to rise, I'm meant to be free.

This world may try to clip your flight,
Hold back your steps and dim your light.
But take one stride, break through the haze,
And show them how a soul can blaze.

13. The Lines I Write

Your mornings bright were never made
To serve in silence, stay afraid.
Your darkest nights still held your spark,
Your dreams alive, though skies were dark.

They tied your hands in unseen chains,
Wrote your fate with borrowed names.
But you were never meant to stay
Bound by the lines they drew that way.

Clench your fist, and raise it high,
Break the walls and touch the sky.
You are the one who writes your fate,
With fire and grace — bold, innate.

14. Losers Have Many Reasons

They say, "I'll start when the time is right,"
When the stars align, when the mood is light.
But time slips by like grains of sand,
And dreams stay sketches in trembling hands.

They have a plan, or so they claim,
But perfect storms are hard to tame.
They wait for calm, they wait for signs,
They wait so long, they miss the lines.

Fear of failure paints their mind,
"What if I fall? What will they find?"
They build excuses, tall and wide,
And hide their fire deep inside.

They say, "I'm not ready, I need more time,"
"I'll try tomorrow, it'll be fine."
But tomorrows come with the same old song,
And dreams grow quiet, before too long.

They talk of odds, of risk, of fate,
Of all the reasons why they wait.
The world feels harsh, the hill too steep,
So they trade bold steps for restless sleep.

But winners?
They don't wait for stars to shine.
They move with fear, they cross the line.
They leap before they know the way,
They build the bridge along the way.

Losers have many reasons, it’s true—
But none that dreams will listen to.
So start, not perfect, start afraid,
Or spend your life in plans you made.

15. The Man in the Mirror

All his life, he played each part,
With duty etched upon his heart.
In school, he chased the perfect grade,
Burning nights while others laid.

Then college came, he ran again,
Through crowded roads and pouring rain.
A job, a home, a family's need,
He kept on running at full speed.

He chased his kids with joy and pride,
Held their hands and walked beside.
He crawled on knees so they could stand,
Guiding dreams with steady hand.

He tasted lies, he faced deceit,
Sometimes with loss, sometimes defeat.
Yet through the storms, he wore a smile,
And pushed himself that extra mile.

But time, it walks with silent grace,
And one day, he just saw his face...
In the mirror, standing still,
A stranger shaped by time and will.

He blinked, confused, "Is this still me?"
Where's the boy I used to be?
The laughter, dreams, that fearless fire...
Now buried deep beneath desire.

He'd gained so much along the way,
But lost himself more every day.
And in that glass, it came so clear:
He'd loved and lived... but disappeared.

So hear this truth, both bold and raw:
You can give the world your all in awe.
But don't forget, amidst life's race,
To hold on tight to your own face.

16. In Someone Else's Dream

We came with stars stitched to our skies,
With wild hopes dancing in our eyes,
Sketching futures in shades so bold,
Dreams too tender, dreams too gold.

But life—it speaks in softer tones,
In quiet sighs, in aging bones.
And sometimes paths begin to bend,
When love becomes the journey's end.

I had a dream, I held it tight,
Lit by ambition's burning light.
But then I saw your dream unfold,
And it felt warmer than my own gold.

To see you smile, to see you shine,
To make your victories feel like mine,
I placed my dreams upon a shelf,
And found a joy outside myself.

It isn't loss, it isn't pain,
To stand outside and feel the rain,
Of someone else's grateful eyes,
And call that moment my sunrise.

Because life is more than just our name,
More than fortune, more than fame.
It's in the love we choose to give,
In helping someone else to live.

And so I walk this path unseen,
Inside the light of your bright dream.
It may not be what I once planned.
But it's still magic, hand in hand.

It's all about the joy we sow,
The peace in letting your dream grow.
It's all about love—pure and true,
And if it's for you... it's my dream too.

17. Touch the Sky, Walk the Earth

Away from the crowd, I choose my pace,
Not in a hurry, not in a race.
While others chase the shine and show,
I walk the path where real things grow.

I dream to touch the endless sky,
But never let my roots run dry.
For what is flight without the land?
A drifting kite, without command.

I rise with work, I build, I strive,
I feel the world, I feel alive.
Gold may glitter in my hand,
But I still love the feel of sand.

No crown is real if worn with pride,
If ego walks, then grace must hide.
So even when I reach the stars,
I count my steps; I heal my scars.

For I have seen, in life's own game,
A single wave can drown your name.
Fortunes fall like castles made,
On shores where once you danced and played.

So, walk with heart, not just head,
Let kindness guide each word you've said.
Touch the sky if that's your way,
But let your soul on earth still stay.

18. Desire & Require

In the garden of dreams where wild winds blow,
A young heart stands with a silent "no."
One hand holds stars, the other holds stone,
Between desire and require, he walks alone.

Desire is a fire that dances in eyes,
It paints futures under midnight skies.
It whispers, "Be bold, be free, just try..."
It sings in verses, it dares to fly.

Require is the weight that anchors the soul,
It speaks in spreadsheets, in daily tolls.
It says, "Be wise, be safe, survive..."
It builds the walls where dreams won't thrive.

Youth is a war between wish and need,
Between the poems we write and the paths we heed.
You want to paint, but you fix the wires,
You dream of oceans, but clock in for hours.

They don't teach this battle in school halls bright,
The silent ache of giving up flight.
The art you loved, the words you wrote,
They fade beneath bills, beneath rent, beneath coat.

Because life, oh life, she plays unfair,
She gives you wings, then cages air.
She gives you desire in full display,
But demands require to lead the way.

How cruel it is: to want, yet pause,
To bury your spark for a greater cause.
To smile at duty while your soul still grieves,
To water gardens you'll never see leaves.

But here's the truth, raw and bare—
Desire may flicker, but it's always there.
And sometimes, in quiet, between the lines,
It sneaks into work, it softly shines.

So, if you must choose, and most times you will,
Let require be your bridge, but desire your will.
Balance the weight with the light in your chest,
And never forget what made your heart rest.

19. A dawn that never came

Every night will test your will,
Push you harder, break you still.
You don't know what lies ahead,
What new battles must be bled...

Go and ask the ones who wait,
For a dawn that never came...

Dreams will rise, dreams will fade,
Hope will walk a step ahead.
But ask the hearts that lost their way,
For them, the sun won't shine today.

Life will weave a dream so bright,
A spark of hope, a guiding light.
But shadows hide in silent pain,
Some will wait, but not remain.

Go and ask the ones who pray,
For a dawn that never came...

Wishes whispered in the night,
Some take flight, some lose sight...
Dreams once born for morning's glow,
Stay in eyes, but never grow...

But someday light will find its way,
Somewhere far, there'll be a day...
And if you see them lost in time,
Tell them, morning is on its way.

20. Wait for the Sunrise

When the night feels long and the pain feels wide,
When every smile is just something you hide,
And silence screams louder than any sound,
You wonder if peace is six feet underground.

But listen, dear soul, before you decide,
There's more to you than the tears you cried.
Death has a day—it will find its way,
But not today. No, **not today**.

Some people died with dreams still whole,
Crushed by fate, not by their soul.
They didn't choose the final breath,
It came unasked, it brought their death.

A child was laughing, crossing the lane,
Gone in a flash, just like rain.
They didn't want to leave this place,
Yet life can vanish with no trace.

And still, there are those who stayed and fought,
Who lost it all but never forgot—
The girl who climbed Everest with no real feet,
The boy with no arms who still chased beat.

Medals hung where wounds once bled,
They chose to live when hope had fled.
They too had nights with heavy eyes,
But they rose with fire, they chose to rise.

You say you're tired, I hear you clear,
But giving up now? Don't you dare.
Remember the dream that made your heart race,
Can you truly leave it without a taste?

Failure isn't yours to own,
It visits all, and then it's gone.
But chances? Oh, they're like stars,
Scattered far, but always ours.

Abort that thought that ends the tale,
It's just a storm, you're not that frail.
And years from now, you'll sit in light,
Thankful you chose to win that fight.

So, stay. For the book you'll write one day.
For the child who'll laugh your way.

For the stage, the song, the lover, the friend,
For the story that didn't have to end.

You are more than your darkest part,
There's still music in your heart.
So breathe again, take one more stride.
Because the sunrise waits on the other side.

21. Born for More

"What do you want to be?"—they ask with care,
A question we answer with voices rare.
Not for ourselves, but to make them proud,
To please the family, to fit the crowd.

A good son for mom and dad to adore,
A brother who always gives and asks no more.
For uncles and aunts—we wear the smile,
Polite and perfect, all the while.
For society—we play the role,
Of calm, cultured, a selfless soul.

We become so much for everyone's sake,
But what about the dreams we never wake?

Have you ever paused and asked within,
What would I be, if life were mine to begin?

Why is it when it's time to choose,
We pick just one and let others lose?

Can’t I be an engineer—and love the stage?
Code the future—and still engage
In acting out a fearless part,
With science in mind and fire in heart?

Can’t a doctor swim wild seas too?
With healing hands and a sky so blue.
Can’t a lawyer stand firm in court by day,
And still roam free on mountain way?

Why must dreams fight for space?
Why can't passion set the pace?
Why do we shrink to just one name,
When we were born to play more than one game?

You can be many things, not just one—
The moon, the mountain, and the sun.
So next time they ask, “*What will you be?*”
Say, **“Everything life planted in me.”**